Contents

Introduction

Movement is one of a child's first means of expression, of communication and of learning about the world. By observing children from an early age, we see abundant evidence of their natural love of movement in their spontaneous jumping, whirling, hopping and running.

Young children show their feelings immediately in the way they move. In providing opportunities for dance and movement in the Foundation Stage, we are harnessing the child's natural ability to use the language of movement for creative expression.

Dance and movement education is crucial to the development of the whole child and is a vital part of the Foundation Stage Curriculum. It is an integral aspect of creative development that makes a valuable contribution to children's understanding of the world around them.

We know from recent research into the development of the human brain that it is essential to provide children with opportunities to develop both hemispheres of the brain.

'Before children can learn the complex skills of reading and writing, they need to make hundreds of thousands of links between the left side of the brain and the right side of the brain, through the "super highway" of the brain called the corpus callosum. In order to develop these essential links between left and right hemispheres, children need to be involved in activities using both sides of their bodies – both hands, both feet, both eyes, both ears....'

Ros Bayley and Sally Featherstone, 'Smooth Transitions'

As Ros Bayley and Sally Featherstone also point out:

'Recent studies have also shown a correlation between beat competency and school achievement.'

Dance and movement sessions also have a major contribution to make towards the development of the brain and of beat competency. This book will help you to provide the creative and physical possibilities of dance in your setting.

The Little Book of Dance

Dance activities for the Foundation Stage

Written by
Julie Quinn and Naomi Wager

Illustrations by Martha Hardy

LITTLE BOOKS WITH BIG IDEAS

Published 2009 by A&C Black Publishers Limited
36 Soho Square, London W1D 3QY
www.acblack.com

First published in the UK by Featherstone Education Limited 2004

ISBN 9871904187745

Text © Julie Quinn and Naomi Wager, 2004
Illustrations © Martha Hardy, 2004
Series Editor Sally Featherstone

Printed in Great Britain by Latimer Trend & Company Limited

This book is produced using paper that is made from wood grown in
managed, sustainable forests. It is natural, renewable and recyclable.

The logging and manufacturing processes conform to the environmental
regulations of the country of origin.

**To see our full range of titles
visit www.acblack.com**

Getting Started

Starting a new activity is always a bit of a strain! But some simple preparation will make the sessions easier to manage and will allow you to be more spontaneous. Children respond well to short activities. Sometimes these can be used to enhance stories, rhymes and other focus activities you have already planned; at other times you may want to use a simple dance activity to make a natural break in the day, to help children to let off steam, or just for fun! Remember, little and often works best. A warm-up activity and an action poem may be enough for younger children. You could then add a simple movement sequence and a relaxation activity as they get used to the sessions and develop their concentration skills.

Collect some simple resources

The following resources and equipment will provide a starter to your collection. Put them in a special box, basket or small trolley so they are available whenever you need them. If you have to spend time looking for the music CD or a tambourine, you may lose the moment of inspiration!

Simple musical instruments could include:

a small drum   a tambourine
'jingle' bells   a rain stick
a wave drum for sea sounds   maracas
simple shakers (home-made ones are fine) and castanets

These will help you to regain the children's attention and to help to suggest the different types, characters and speeds of movements.

Other resources could include:

▶ some lengths of light, stretchy fabric (about 2–3 metres each) in various colours; blue, brown and green are specially useful.
▶ ribbons and streamers, some on short sticks.
▶ a small collection of music on tape and CD (CD makes it much easier to find the track you need). Include a variety of music, for example, pop, classical, dance and world music. Concentrate on pieces of music with a clear beat, strong rhythm and a range of moods.

Links with the Early Learning Goals for the Foundation Stage

The Early Learning Goals linked to Dance and to the activities suggested in this book are:

Personal and Social Development

▶ Respond to significant experiences, showing a range of feelings when appropriate.

▶ Work as part of a group or class, taking turns and sharing fairly, understanding that there need to be agreed values and codes of behaviour for groups of people, including adults and children, to work together harmoniously.

Language, Communication and Literacy

▶ Listen with enjoyment and respond to stories, songs and other music, rhymes and poems and make up their own stories, songs, rhymes and poems.

▶ Use language to imagine and recreate roles and experiences.

Mathematical Development

▶ Use everyday words to describe position.

Knowledge and Understanding of the World

▶ Begin to know about their own cultures and beliefs and those of other people.

Physical Development

▶ Move with confidence, imagination and in safety.

▶ Move with control and coordination.

▶ Show awareness of space, of themselves and of others.

▶ Recognise the importance of keeping healthy and those things which contribute to this.

▶ Recognise the changes that happen to their bodies when they are active.

Creative Development

▶ Recognise and explore how sounds can be changed, sing simple songs from memory, recognise repeated sounds and sound patterns, and match movements to music.

▶ Use their imagination in art and design, music, dance, imaginative role-play and stories.

▶ Respond in a variety of ways to what they see, hear, smell, touch and feel.

▶ Express and communicate their ideas, thoughts and feelings by using a widening range of materials, suitable tools, imaginative role-play, movement, designing and making, and a variety of songs and musical instruments.

Using the book

The purpose of this Little Book is to provide you with ideas to inspire dance sessions.

The ideas have been organised into three sections:

1. Seasonal themes

2. Cultural themes

3. Using books as a starting point.

Each dance session contains detailed guidance on what you could say as well as what you could do. Guidance on what to say is printed in a contrasting colour. This guidance is for you to take and use as you wish.

You could:

▶ follow it closely

▶ pick and choose from the range of suggestions

▶ develop your own 'script' using the guidance as a starting point.

The important thing is to feel confident, to enjoy yourself and to relax into the activity. Some children may be reluctant to join in at first. If this is the case, go slowly, do frequent short sessions and above all, have fun!

Warm-up Activities

Every session should start with a warm-up. This activity signals the start of the session, helps children to relax and warms up their bodies. Choose one of these activities to start your sessions. The children will soon develop favourites that they will request time after time.

The 'Hello' Song

It is reassuring for children to have a simple 'signature tune' to begin each session. You could sing:

Hello children,
Hello children,
Hello children,
Come and dance with me.

You could sing your 'Hello' song to a familiar tune, such as a nursery rhyme or popular song. Using this as a framework, you can make up your own words, include some simple actions begin to introduce basic movement vocabulary. Add a new verse or a new movement when you feel the children are ready.

It is also a good idea to finish your dance session with a 'Goodbye' song. Repetitive, predictable elements allow every child to succeed and develop confidence in their own ability.

Two of the tracks on the CD accompanying this book are particularly good for warm-up activities – they are Sand Dance and Desert Rain.

A Goodbye Song
– (to 'Twinkle Twinkle Little Star')

Goodbye children, how time flies,
Now it's time to say goodbye,
We have stretched up to the sky,
Run and jumped and tried to fly,
I hope you have had some fun,
Now the end of dancing's come.

Movement Warm-ups

All children enjoy games much better if you can combine a lively activity with some movement ideas that will develop movement vocabulary and require some movement memory.

Busy Beans Warm-Up

The children travel in the space, looking around and being careful not to collide with others. On your command they perform the following actions:

Chilli beans	shiver/shake as if you are very cold.
Runner beans	run quickly on the spot.
Jumping beans	bounce on the move or on the spot.
Baked beans	melt to the floor as if you're melting.
Jelly beans	wobble.
Broad beans	make a wide shape.

The Dice Game

Using a small box or a soft cube with pockets that you can slide pictures in, draw or insert a body part on each face of the cube (arms, hands, feet, head, body, legs etc.).

▶ Ask one child to hold the cube in the middle of the room while the others move around the space to a clapping rhythm. You can stipulate the mode of travel e.g. hopping, jumping etc.

▶ On your cue, everyone stops and the child with the cube throws it to reveal a body part.

▶ The children must hold up, wave or put that part on the floor.

Action Rhymes and Poems

Action songs, rhymes and poems make good starting points and are excellent 'ice breakers' with a new group. Children will feel comfortable with their familiarity, which is a sort of 'half way house' requiring some active participation but in a familiar context. It is usually possible to find an action rhyme to complement your theme and all of the ideas in this book suggest action rhymes as an introduction to the main focus of the session.

Here is one example. There are ideas for more at the beginning of each dance theme in the book.

Thin as a pin

▶ **Thin as a pin**   Stand on your toes, arms stretched high above your head, stretch, and stretch, stretch!

▶ **Wide as a house**   Make the widest shape you can manage.

▶ **Round as a ball**   Soften your knees, curve your spine and cuddle a massive beach ball.

▶ **Small as a mouse**   Make yourself as small as possible on the floor, tuck up tight then scamper and squeak.

Movement-based Ideas

It is sometimes useful to try out new ideas that you intend to use in the session as part of your warm-up, just to see how the children respond.

Sometimes, when children are working on themes that develop their creativity, they get so absorbed in the idea that you do not achieve the quality and variety of movement that you were hoping.

It can be useful to focus on these aspects as part of the opening activity and warm-up.

The example opposite focuses on experiencing a variety of movement qualities and developing spatial awareness through familiar story characters.

Using Mr Men characters as a stimulus

Some of the 'Mr Men' characters (and the companion 'Miss' stories) have great movement potential. Use pictures or the books to remind children, or ask them to guess who the characters are. Some examples are:

Mr Slow

Can you walk like Mr Slow?
Can you sit down like Mr Slow?
How would Mr Slow stretch?
How would he roll over?
Can you get up like Mr Slow?

Mr Bounce

How does Mr Bounce walk?
Can he bounce forwards, sideways
and backwards?
Using hoops try straight bounces and zigzag bounces
Can you bounce on one leg?
With feet together and apart? Try alternating them.
Try bouncing while you turn around.

Over several weeks you might also explore:

Mr Jelly	Miss Late
Mr Tall and Mr Small	Miss Busy
Mr Rush	Miss Tiny
Mr Strong	Miss Shy
Mr Clumsy	Miss Bossy

Or you could move like:

'The Tiger who Came to Tea'
'Elmer the Elephant'
Animals in the jungle, at the farm or zoo
Underwater creatures
Dinosaurs, insects and toys.

Roots and Shoots

Seasonal dance – spring

> Start your dance session with a welcome and warm-up activity from **Section 1**.

What you need

- ▶ a watering can
- ▶ a packet of seeds or some seeds you have collected
- ▶ the book **The Tiny Seed** by Eric Carle
- ▶ small mats or carpet tiles
- ▶ a tambourine

Music suggestion

- ▶ **Awakening** by Brian Madigan
  (track 1 on the 'Music for Dance' CD)

Action poems

- ▶ This is the Sun
- ▶ A Bee in my Garden

Opening activity

Follow your-warm up with these two action poems to get in the mood and to give the children a clue about the theme of today's dance.

This is the Sun

This is the sun,

circular shape with arms
above head

So big and round.

This is a seed,

tight small shape on the ground

So snug in the ground.

These are the flowers,

kneeling arms wave overhead

That wave in the breeze.

These are the yachts,

standing, turn around with one hand
on hip and the other stretched high

That sail on the seas.

A Bee in my Garden

There's a bee in my garden.

It's buzzing away zzzzzz.

I wonder where it will find

Nectar today.

The children sit in a circle. One
weaves in and out of the circle as if
visiting flowers.

He/she then stops and touches one
of the group who then becomes the
next bee – sound effects welcome!

Setting the scene for the dance

What do you think?

Gather the group together and introduce the theme through lots of discussion and sharing of experiences and ideas – this is always a good way to put children at ease and get them involved.

Some prompts:

▷ Who can tell me what season of the year we are in? Has anyone noticed anything different about the trees on their way to school, nursery or playgroup?

▷ Has anyone got any flowers or bulbs coming up in their garden at the moment?

▷ Have you noticed how cheerful the birds seem to be?

▷ It's the time of year for growth and new life and we are going to work on some ideas about that.

Developing your idea

Some suggested prompts:

- ▶ Come and collect a magic mat and go and plant it in the garden.

- ▶ Your mat is a flower. Remember not to plant it close to any other mat, as it will need space to grow.

- ▶ Move like a bee in and out of the mats while the tambourine shimmies. When it stops, hover over one of the beautiful mat flowers, stand on one leg, stare at something to help you stay still and stretch your arms out to the side to help you. Repeat this several times.

- ▶ Play the tambourine again. This time, you are a grasshopper (or a frog). Jump over the mat like this. Demonstrate if they need it.

- ▶ Now you are a garden pest, coming to eat the flowers!
  You are a slippery, slimy, slow-moving snail. Slither slowly back to me.

Creating a dance

Gather the group together to discuss plans for the group dance.

Here are some prompts:

- ▶ Who knows what is in this little packet?
  Shake the seed packet.

- ▶ Where do the seeds come from? (Not the garden centre!) I expect some of you have grown sunflowers before, and looked at the seed heads when the petals have died.

- ▶ What do seeds need so they can grow?
  Give clues – hold up the watering can, make the 'big round sun' movement from the action poem, and talk about the warm soil.

- ▶ We're going to look at the journey of a tiny seed and how it becomes a beautiful plant and flower.

A possible dance structure: What you could say

1. Snuggle down in the soil like a tiny seed. Older or more experienced dancers could try to make a pattern like a sunflower seed head by arranging their curled bodies in circles.

2. Now I'm going to be the wind. When you hear me huffing and puffing the seeds are going to get blown away. Tuck up tight and practice rolling along the ground.

3. Now all the seeds have found a comfortable place to settle. Snuggle into the soil while the soft rain waters you. Use the watering can to water the resting seed so they begin to grow.

4. Now the seeds are full of water. They are starting to get bigger and bigger until they are ready to burst like little balloons.

5. The seeds are ready to send out wriggly roots, burrowing down into the soil. They get all knotted and tangled and they twist around other roots. Encourage the children to use a variety of body parts as the roots. They could work together to twine round each other's roots. The movements could include flexible, weaving, wavy actions done near the floor or high up.

6. The roots are growing strongly in the warm earth; now the shoots are ready to push through the surface of the soil and burst out towards the sunlight. Suggest that these movements could be sharp and angular, and the shoot may grow in surges and stages. The hands could lead this movement, representing the shoot.

7. From a small tight bud made by your hands, a flower slowly unfolds. Use your fingers to show the petals unfolding. The second flower is even better. Use your whole body to open out into a bigger and better bloom. Try starting with your body crouched low and tucked in; now open out into a wide body shape.

8. Now at last the flower is wilting and fading as the petals softly float to the ground.
If the children are ready for more, you could discuss how the cycle of life begins again as the new seeds start to form.

Chocofrolics

Seasonal dance – Easter

Start your dance session with a welcome and warm-up activity from **Section 1**, or one you have invented.

What you need

- a box of chocolates or a filled Easter egg
- small mats or carpet tiles
- a tambourine

Music suggestion

- **Just a Spoonful of Sugar** from Mary Poppins

Action poems

- Five Little Eggs
- Crackly Egg

Opening activity

Follow your chosen warm-up with these two action poems so the children have a clue about the theme of the dance today – eggs and chocolate.

Five Little Eggs

Five little eggs all speckled and white,

Extend fingers on right hand.

Side by side in their nest.

Cup hand, close fist.

Out popped the head of the first little chick,

Thumb pops out.

Out popped the heads of the rest!

Other fingers pop out, one by one.
Repeat with left hand.

Crackly Egg

Little chicken in the egg,

Quiet as quiet can be.

Clench thumb in fist.

Crackle, crackle, crackle, crack.

Rotate fist back and forth.

Out pops she!

Setting the scene for the dance

What do you think?

Gather the children together and introduce the theme through lots of discussion and sharing of experiences and ideas about Easter eggs and other food for celebrations.

Some prompts:

▶ We're all going to be enjoying a holiday soon. Who can tell me what we might be eating over the holiday a special treat that we only have at this time of year?

▶ At this time of year people sometimes send cards or make cards at school. These cards often have furry animals on them. Which animals are they?

▶ Well, today we're going to start by learning how to hop just like an Easter bunny. Can you do some bunny hops?

Developing your idea

Spread small mats around the space and teach the basic bunny hop.
You could say:

▶ You do bunny hops like this – bend down and put your hands on the mat. Reach forward as far as you can without falling over! Now without lifting your hands, can you jump your feet to meet your hands?

▶ Now walk all round the room without stepping on any of the mats. When I stop shaking the tambourine and bang it, find the nearest mat and do a bunny hop over it.

Now teach them how to rock.

▶ Hug your knees and tuck your head into your chest.
Now rock like an egg. Try rocking until you rock yourself onto your feet.

▶ Now walk between the mats and when I stop shaking the tambourine and bang it, find a mat to rock on like an oval Easter egg.

Creating a dance

Gather the group together to discuss plans for the group dance.

Here are some prompts for your discussion:

▶ What do you think is in this box?
Show them the box of chocolates and then open it and look inside.

▶ Let's look at the names of all the chocolates and choose our favourites.
Find the description sheet and talk about all the different chocolates in your box. Let each child say which is their favourite.

▶ In our dance, we are going to turn into chocolates – all the different sorts.

▶ Pretend you are eating your favourite chocolate. Put it in your mouth and think about the taste and how it feels on your tongue.

A possible dance structure: What you could say

1. Let's try out some chocolate movements all together. Here comes a Hazelnut Swirl! *Practice swirling and turning from up high to low*.

2. Now let's try some more. Try nutty clusters curled up tight then breaking open when someone takes a bite; or a caramel wave, swooping across the room, making wave actions with your arms; or a melting strawberry cream, standing up high then melting to the floor as you slowly say 'strawberry cream!'; or a chocolate cherry, curled up with your arms over your head, then slowly breaking out of the chocolate covering.

3. Now let's put all the mats together so they can be a box and we can be the chocolates. *Collect up the mats and put them in two or three rows like the rows in a chocolate box*.

4. Choose a place and get into the chocolate box sections.

5. When I play the tambourine, rise out of your box and be all the different chocolates. You choose which one you will be.

6. And to finish, we will all be those chocolate Easter eggs. Sit on a mat and rock like a big fat Easter egg.

7. When I bang the tambourine, start to crack and break into pieces on the floor.

8. Try again and this time, start rocking, and as I shake the tambourine, melt into a big pool of chocolate – as big as you can make yourself!

Splash Dance

Seasonal dance – summer

This is a long session and some of the activities are more suitable for older children. You will need to use your judgement and select the ideas that will suit your children's age, concentration and interest. Younger children could cover the material over several sessions.

What you need

- hoops
- a long rope or ribbon
- swimming props – swim ring, towel, goggles, swim toys etc.
- the book **The Tiny Seed** by Eric Carle
- small mats or carpet tiles
- a tambourine

Music suggestion

- A **Sea Sounds** CD

Action poem

- Upon a Beach

Opening activity

Follow your chosen warm-up with this simple action poem so the children can guess what the theme of the dance is today.

Upon a Beach

The children sit in a circle. Choose three of them to be shells and five others to be waves, holding hands.

Verse 1:
Upon a beach
Three small shells lay,
The three shells lie on the beach.
And saw the water
Come out to play.
The waves come and skip around them, holding hands.

Verse 2:
But, all the waves
Went back to sea,
The waves take the shells by the hand.
And took those shells,
One, two and three.
And take them back to the sea.

You could repeat the rhyme several times so all the children can have a turn at being shells and waves.

Setting the scene for the dance

Talk to the children about the sort of activities they enjoy doing in the summer. Someone is sure to mention swimming. Ask about swimming in the sea – has anyone ever done it?

Some prompts:

▶ Do you like swimming in the sea? Is it better than swimming in a pool?

▶ Do you like splashing?

▶ Do you like going under water? Can you swim under the water?

▶ What does the beach feel like under your feet? Is it sand? Stones? Rocks? Seaweed?

▶ What does the sea smell like? What does it look like? How far can you see from the beach? What do the waves sound like?

▶ Let's look at some swimming things.
Ask the children to take turns to dip into the bag and remove arm bands, swim ring, snorkel, goggles, swimming costumes etc.

Developing your idea

Using a hoop each as a seaside pool, try the following ideas. Here are some prompts of what you could say:

▶ How cold is the water in your pool? Are you going to just jump in, or do you need to dip your toes in first? Try the water and see how it feels.

▶ Now run to your pool and jump in with a splash. Try to land on two feet to make a really big splash! Repeat several times.

▶ Imagine you have made a big splash and jump high out of the water like an exploding fountain. You could make a sound as you jump - try whooshsh!

▶ Now creep slowly and nervously towards the pool, perhaps shiver a bit as you dip your toe in. Maybe you could take a few steps back and then try the other toe and then your fingers. Pretend the pool is really cold.

Underwater

Talk about how the children feel about going underwater.

▶ Do you like going under water? Or is it a bit scary?

▶ Let's jump into our swimming pools holding our noses. Then we can sink right down to the bottom.
Encourage a weightless, floaty sort of movement as they slowly drift downwards. Use soft fluid arm and hand movements, stress the sustained and continuous character of the movement. Suggest some sound effects, such as bubble blowing noises.

▶ What does it feel like to walk underwater along the bottom of the pool? It's hard to move quickly; try walking in slow motion, moving very smoothly.

▶ Now come up for air and stretch up to the surface with one big stroke. Take a deep breath and then sink down again.

Swimming strokes (an extension for older children)

Talk about swimming strokes and ask the children to demonstrate the ones they can do.

▶ Show everyone how to do breast stroke arms and ask them to copy the pattern. Exaggerate the size of the stroke and ask for large sweeping arm actions. Also show them a side stroke on both sides of the body and build into a repetitive movement pattern e.g. four basic breast strokes then two quick side strokes, right then left.

▶ Remind the group of what backstroke arms do. Draw large backward circles with your arms, keeping them very close to your body and completing a full circle, remaining stretched throughout. Make sure the arms are moved alternately and fairly slowly to allow for the fullness of movement. The children could copy you and then travel carefully and slowly around the space, walking backwards and watching carefully to avoid other swimmers.

▶ Lie on the floor face down and ask if anyone can demonstrate what to do with your arms when you swim front crawl.
Who can make the biggest splash with their feet? See if you can get your friend wet! Practice the crawl action with your arms and legs.

Diving!

▶ Have you ever done a dive into the swimming pool? We are going to try a sort of dive in our dance. Begin by kneeling and then try to slide forwards along the floor. Make your body long and stretched and finish with a few swimming strokes with your arms.

▶ Now try some different sorts of dive:

A high dive: start crouched then stretch upwards with your arms before plunging into the pool.

A racing dive: swing your arms from behind before sliding along the floor.

Getting dry

- ▶ Has anyone got a dog? Can you show us how your dog gets dry after a swim? Shall we try shaking like the dog?
  Shake your hands and feet, each one separately, then together. Shake each shoulder, then both together. Shake and wiggle your bottom. Now shake your whole body.
- ▶ We could do a shaking, drying dance. Walk around your hoop like this: step, step, shake, shake, shake, step, step, shake, shake, shake.
- ▶ Hold your towel stretched out in both hands and rub behind your neck, back and bottom in a rhythm. Change the rhythm and rub different parts of your body.
- ▶ Now let's get dressed again. What do we need to put on first? Let's start by peeling off our wet swimsuits. They stick don't they?
- ▶ Now struggle into your sweatshirt, popping your head quickly through the hole. Reach down and carefully put your feet into your warm snuggly socks and slowly stretch them up your legs.

Soaking up the sun

- ▶ As a calming activity at the end of the session, you could introduce the idea of sunbathing and relaxing by the pool.
- ▶ Talk about how to keep safe in the sun. Begin by asking them to apply imaginary sun cream all over their bodies and then ask the children to spread out their towels and assume their favourite and most comfortable 'snoozing' position.
- ▶ Suggest changes of position, finding different ways of relaxing – on tummies, sides and sitting up. Try flicking through a book, taking a long cool drink, mopping your brow, falling asleep, stretching etc.
  Use some soothing, tranquil music as a background.

A possible dance structure: What you could say

Having explored some or all of the ideas suggested, you may want to put the movements together and perform them to music. Let the children help you to arrange the hoops or a long skipping rope or ribbon into a large swimming pool shape. Begin with the children away from the pool you have made.

1. As the music begins, creep towards the pool and test the water. Move back, then try again and take the plunge, jumping in, holding your nose.

2. Sink to the bottom of the pool and explore underwater, circling around the pool and moving in slow motion.

3. Now kneel in the pool and start to swim the breast stroke, with your arms going to the front and side.

4. Turn over so that you are sitting on your bottom outside the pool and do some splashing with your feet in the water. Try varying the force and rhythm of the kicking actions, using the tambourine as a prompt.

5. Now stand up in the pool and slowly turn around until you are in a space of your own, turning all the time. Swim carefully around the pool. Don't swim into anyone else.

6. Try swimming backwards, using your backstroke and looking out for other swimmers.

7. Come out of the pool again and get ready to practise your diving. Take care not to dive on anyone else. You could use the tambourine to help with the diving, banging it, then shaking the jingles for the splashes.

8. Time to get out. Climb out of the pool and shake your arms, legs, feet and hands to shake off the water. Now pick up your towel and start to dry yourself.

9. Spread out your towel and sit on it to put on your sun cream. Lie down on your towel and soak up the sun!

In Our Yellow Submarine

Seasonal dance – summer

This session builds on the splash dance. It gives children an opportunity to repeat and develop swimming and diving movements in a fantasy sequences of diving for treasure.

What you need

- a box for treasure
- old, cheap or toy jewellery, coins etc. for treasure
- the book **What's Under the Sea?** (Usborne Pocket Science)
- a toy submarine (if possible)
- goggles, masks, snorkels etc.

Music suggestion

- **The Yellow Submarine** by The Beatles

Action poem

- Four Little Divers

Opening activity

Choose a warm-up activity to start the session and follow it with this action rhyme.

Four Little Divers

The children sit in a circle. Choose four divers, one shark, one octopus and one jellyfish. The divers 'dive' into the circle and swim round as you begin the poem.

Verse 1:
Four little divers
Swimming out to sea,
One met a shark!
And then there were three.
The shark takes a diver back to the circle of children.

Verse 2:
Three little divers
Wondered what to do,
One met an octopus,
And then there were two.
The octopus grabs a diver and takes them back to the circle.

Verse 3:
Two little divers
Looking for some fun,
One met a jellyfish,
And then there was one.
The jellyfish grabs one diver and takes them to the circle.

Verse 4:
One little diver
Swimming all alone,
He swam back home again
And then there were none.
The last diver swims round the circle and returns to their place.

You could repeat the rhyme several times so all the children have a turn at being divers and creatures.

Setting the scene for the dance

What do you think?

▶ What do you know about what happens under the sea?
  Show them the treasure box and look at the contents.

▶ Look at all this diving equipment. Shall we try some on?

▶ Listen to this music about a Yellow Submarine. Let's sing and clap along. Or we could play pretend instruments in a Yellow Submarine Band.

▶ Today we are all going in a submarine for a journey under the sea.

▶ But first we need to practise diving and swimming underwater, sinking and swimming in the deep sea and using flippers to make us swim smoothly underwater.

Developing your idea

▶ Come and practice diving and rising all together. Hold your nose with one hand, hold the other arm up high and slowly sink down to the floor. Now come slowly up again.

▶ Now let's make a boat shape all together, sitting on the floor. Practice rocking together as the waves come. You could use a wave drum or a rain stick to simulate wave sounds, or use a sea sounds tape.

▶ We could make a band in a boat by playing instruments as the band music plays.

▶ Now practice swimming like sea creatures – an octopus, a jellyfish, a starfish, little fishes, a sea anemone and a shark.

Creating a dance

Work with the children to make up an underwater dance.

Here are some ideas for movements:

▶ Diving down in the submarine.

▶ Floating around in the submarine, singing the song.

▶ Putting on your underwater diving kit – wetsuits, goggles, flippers and breathing apparatus.

▶ Swimming out of the submarine in underwater kit and using flippers to swim about under the water – rising up and sinking down in a group or separately.

▶ Some children could be underwater creatures, while others swim among them, taking photos with underwater cameras.

▶ Get back into the submarine and float up to the surface.

▶ Take off the diving gear and climb out of the submarine.

And a relaxation activity

Sit with your feet in imaginary waves as you listen to wave music or sing some sea songs.

Autumn Weather

Seasonal dance – autumn

This dance session could follow an autumn walk in your local park or the garden. Collect some leaves and seeds to look at and use for movement.

What you need

▶ autumn leaves of different sizes, shapes and colours
▶ the books **Autumn** by Pauline Cartwright (Shortland), **Autumn** by Nicola Baxter (Franklin Watts) and **Autumn** by Karen Bryant Mole (Heinemann)

Music suggestion

▶ **A Rainy Day** by Brian Madigan (track 2 on the Music for Dance CD)

Action poems

▶ Up in a Tree
▶ Autumn Leaves

Opening activity

Follow your chosen warm-up with these action poems to help the children to get in the mood for the theme of the dance.

Up in a Tree

Five brown leaves hung.
When the wind came along,
They swung and swung.
Suddenly, without a sound,
One little leaf (or the last little leaf)
Fell to the ground.

Say the verse using five fingers first, then say it again with five children in the middle of the circle, swinging in the wind and taking turns to fall to the ground.

As usual, you could repeat the rhyme several times so all the children can have a turn at being falling leaves.

Autumn Leaves

Little leaves, little leaves,
High up in the trees.
Little leaves, little leaves,
Swinging in the breeze.
Autumn comes along,
And they change from red to brown.
Autumn comes along,
And they flutter to the ground.

Developing your idea

Let the children show you how the leaves move when they fall from the trees.

- ▶ Can you make your body flutter and float slowly down to the ground?
- ▶ Can you twist and turn like a leaf when it's spinning down?
- ▶ Have you noticed what happens to the leaves when the wind blows them along the ground? Can you move like that?
- ▶ Move all over and across the space, lifting up and down with small, quick light movements as the wind blows you around.

Creating a dance
using **A Rainy Day** from the CD

1. Imagining that the rain is falling, run along, catching the raindrops with your hands as they fall.
2. At first the drops fall slowly. Catch them in your hands as you walk. Watch them fall and splash on your fingers and hands.
3. The drops are falling faster now. You will have to walk faster; maybe you need to run. See how many you can catch now.
4. Here comes the wind! Imagine it is making you sway, gently from side to side.
5. The wind is blowing harder. Travel across the floor as if the wind is blowing you in different directions. Travel high and low.
6. Move like the leaves do as they fall from the trees. Use appropriate movement words as the children dance: spinning, turning, floating and fluttering.
7. Remember how the wind blew you across the ground until finally you lie still and flat on the ground.

Fireworks

Seasonal dance – Autumn

This is a long session and some of the activities are more suitable for older children. You will need to use your judgement and select the ideas that will suit your children's age, concentration and interest.
Younger children could cover the material over several sessions, or you could always choose some of the activities for a shorter dance.

What you need

- hoops for 'launch pads'
- a 'guy' for the bonfire
- books **Fireman Sam** and **The Fireworks** (Heinemann)
- percussion instruments – wood block, cymbal, bells, shakers, tambourine etc.

Music suggestion

- **Summer** from the Four Seasons by Vivaldi

Action poems

- The Fireworks
- November the Fifth – by Leonard Clark (excerpts included in text)

Opening activity

This dance needs a lively warm-up as children may be really excited!
Follow it with this action rhyme for everyone to join in.
Use the hoops as launch pads to ensure good spacing.

The Fireworks

Spiky, wiry sparklers
Long and thin and grey.
Mummy lit them with a match
We watched them fizz away.

Whirly twirly Catherine Wheel
Like a spiral snail.
Daddy lit it carefully
As it hung on a nail.

Whizzing, swooping rockets
Flying to the sky,

Can you see them sparkle
Right up there so high?

My sister likes the bangers
But they just make me jump!
Popping, banging all around,
Thump, thump, thump.

My favourite is the Golden Rain
Just stars without a sound,
All the different colours
Falling to the ground.

As usual, you could repeat the rhyme several times so the children
practice the different fireworks several times.

Developing your idea

Talk with the children about:

▶ the noises the fireworks make – whizz, pop, bang and whirr.
▶ the things fireworks do – shoot, explode, spin, whizz, flash,
  sparkle, rise and fall, jump etc.
▶ favourite fireworks.

Explain that today's idea is
going to be a firework dance.

Practice rocket launching

▶ Start with each child in a hoop. Think about what rockets do, and begin by focusing on the launch. Using the countdown is a good way to practise counting skills and the children really enjoy the build up!

▶ Demonstrate and let them practice rolling up from a crouched position with the head unrolling last.

▶ Encourage smooth and fluid movement and try to synchronise the group so they are all about halfway up by '5' and finish on the balls of their feet with arms stretched to the finger tips and above their heads. Some children may need to practise a really long stretch lying on the floor before doing it upright.

Let's practice getting ready to launch

▶ Continue to use the hoops as launch pads. Light the rockets in turn. Ask the children to crouch down in the hoops and explain that you are going to go round to each child to light the rockets.

▶ Suggest that they start their engines and 'rumble and spark' a bit, juddering their bodies and making appropriate sound effects before shooting into the sky.

▶ At the moment of 'lift off', the children should bend their knees to prepare to jump and then shoot explosively into the air. If you practice this several times, you could encourage them to explode in different directions – to the side, jumping backwards, and off one foot rather than two. Show them how to make their fingers pointy and sharp like the nose of the rocket as they launch into the air.

▶ Now the little rockets can fly around the space, weaving in and out of all other rockets. Remind the children to keep their heads up and look around for 'unidentified flying objects'.

▶ Once your rockets have soared through the air, they gradually run out of steam and float softly to the ground.

Ready for more?

If the children are still enjoying the dance, try some different fireworks.

Jumping jacks

▶ Talk about jumping jacks, which are very noisy and full of surprises. They jump in all directions and you never know which way they will go.

▶ Try out different jumping combinations:

▷ Two feet to two feet.

▷ Hopping on right and left foot alternately.

▷ Try turning around as they jump.

▷ Jumping in all directions: forwards, backwards and sideways.

▶ Put the hoops in different patterns on the floor and let individual children jump from hoop to hoop using any of the variations. As each child is jumping, the others might clap to symbolise the 'bang' of the jumping jack.

Check that the floor is not slippery or hoops may skid and cause a fall!

Let's practice getting ready to launch

▶ **Say this rhyme together:**

Catherine wheel, I see how fiercely you spin
Round and round on your pin;
How I admire your circle of fire.

▶ Talk about what a Catherine wheel does. Remind them how it gradually gets faster and faster and spins on the spot. Think about the whirling whizzy noises it makes and encourage vocal sounds as they spin on the spot, gradually increasing speed.

Sparkle and pop, a Roman candle

▶ **Here is another rhyme:**

> I watch how prettily you spark
> Stars in the autumn dark
> Falling like rain, to shoot up again.

▶ Children can use their hands and fingers to perform a firework display of their own.

▶ Can you make your fingers sparkle and twinkle? Make different patterns with your hands as they light up the night sky; reach high and to the sides; try circles with one hand and both hands together; try big patterns and small patterns.

▶ Close your hands up really tight, so they are like a fist. When I clap, shoot your fingers out, as if the firework has popped and exploded. Sometimes do one hand and sometimes do both. Pop in all different directions, sometimes stretching high and sometimes reaching low. Try to make your hands really pointy and sharp. Try to pop quickly and crisply.

▶ You could help younger children to make a dance by adapting some of the ideas in the model on page 38.

Building the bonfire – a group activity for older children

▶ Decide on a site for the bonfire and create a 'twiggy' pyramid shape with the children. Ask them to make their fingers like pointy twigs and find other parts of the body that are similar to the knobbly bits on branches and twigs, like elbows and knees. Try out a few body shapes in isolation and then begin to construct your group bonfire. Begin with their twig shapes lying on the ground.

▶ You could have one child to act as the 'twig collector' who touches the children in turn, to signal that they must travel to the bonfire and add their branch to the class shape. Once all the children are in position, the 'twig collector' can light the fire.

▶ When the bonfire is alight, the children can then represent:

the smoke

Try soft billowing curving pathways with the upper body. Rolling arms and hands, try continuous movement in a variety of directions and levels at a fairly easy slow pace.

and the flames

As a contrast, encourage sudden shooting movements in unexpected directions with sharp fingers. Emphasise speed, introduce some flexible flames but try to bring out different qualities from the smoke.

▶ Finally, choose one child to place an imaginary guy on the bonfire and allow the bonfire to gradually die down as you say this verse:

And you, old guy,
I see how sadly you blaze on,
Till every scrap is gone;
Burnt into ashes,
Your skeleton crashes.

Suggested structure for a bonfire night dance

(using '**Summer**' from The Four Seasons, another suitably dynamic piece of music or a range of percussion instruments played by you or the children).

N.B. Listen to the music together and talk through ideas before you start. Begin with rockets.

1. First, walk around your launch pad (their own hoop) and then settle in the middle and listen for the countdown in the music.

2. Now let's count down as you unroll slowly and rise from your crouched position.

3. Blast off when they hear the flying music – fly, soar, swoosh and jump, remembering to be aware of other people.

4. Prepare for a 'crash landing' as you fall carefully from the sky. You could do this by suddenly dropping like a stone and finishing with a rolling action, or falling gently and slowly to land lightly on the ground.

5. Now become Roman candles rising from the ground into a tall candle shape. Remember how we practiced moving like a Roman candle with flying sparks and little springy jumps. These jumps bring you to the centre for a Catherine wheel formation.

6. Now you break away and spin into a space, using some of the other rotating ideas that we worked on earlier.

7. Next we can become jumping jacks. You might need to remind them of some of the ideas they tried earlier, then select a few children to demonstrate their ideas until a range of different movements have been offered.

8. We can finish our dance with the bonfire idea. After the tiring jumping section, suggest to the children that they settle down on the floor and become brittle dry, spiky twigs.

9. Individually or in groups, the twigs can then be collected and positioned on the bonfire by bonfire builders.

10. The grand finale is the placing of a guy on the top and the leaping flames followed by the gradual dying down of the fire.

The Christmas Cake

Seasonal dance – winter

This is another long session and some of the activities are more suitable for older children. Again, you will need to use your judgement and select the ideas that will suit your children's age, concentration and interest. Younger children could cover the material over several sessions, and you could always choose some of the activities for a shorter dance.

What you need

▶ ingredients and equipment for making a Christmas cake, so children can understand the process and the special vocabulary (bowl, spoon, cherries, apron, baking tin etc.)
▶ books **Christmas Cakes** by Francesca Bosca (North South Books) and **The Jolly Christmas Postman** by Alan Ahlberg (Puffin)

Music suggestion

▶ Christmas music, carols and songs

Action poem

▶ We're Going to Make a Cake (from **This Little Puffin**)

Opening activity

You could use this song as a warm-up activity to get the children in a baking mood! Sing it to the tune of **The Farmer's in his Den**.

We're Going to Make a Cake

The children sit in a circle and follow the movements as they sing the song.

We're going to make a cake,
We're going to make a cake,
We'll make enough for everyone,
We're going to make a cake.

Break a big brown egg,
Break a big brown egg,
Crack the shell and put it in,
Break a big brown egg.

Raisins in the bowl,
Raisins in the bowl,
Stir it with a great big spoon,
Raisins in the bowl.

Cherries go in next,
Cherries go in next,
They are red and round and sweet,
Cherries go in next.

Icing on the top,
Icing on the top,
Spread it with a big flat knife,
Icing on the top.

Decorate the cake,
Decorate the cake,
Put a Christmas tree on top,
Of our Christmas cake.

You could make up more verses and actions with the children.

Setting the scene for the dance

What do you think?

Some prompts for introducing the dance:

▶ Look at all the ingredients in the song. What do you think we might be doing today?

▶ We all like cooking. Have you ever made a cake?

▶ What do we need to make a cake? Let's look at some of the ingredients we need.

▶ We are going to make a pretend Christmas cake today and you are going to be the ingredients!

▶ Let's sit in a circle to make our cakes. Make a bowl shape with your arm and stir round and round with your other hand. Listen to the wave drum (or shaker) so you know how quickly to stir. We've got sugar and butter in the bowl. Can you feel the gritty, sugary mixture?

▶ Now you need to add the eggs, breaking each one on the side of the bowl and opening the shell. This needs both hands, so you will have to put your 'bowls' down on the floor. We need to use six eggs.

The flour dance!

▶ Now let's all be the rest of the ingredients in the cake.

▶ The next ingredient is a light sprinkling of flour. So spin gently to the middle of the area (our great big bowl).

▶ Rise onto your toes and 'sprinkle' with your fingers as you slowly sink to the ground from high to low. You are light and airy, with a floaty feeling as you drift down into the bowl, onto the sugary, buttery, eggy mix.

Round, red, bouncing cherries!

▶ It's time for the cherries! Make yourself into a round shape. The cherries are like little footballs and they are going to bounce into the middle of the bowl. Come back into a circle shape and be ready to bounce into the mixture. Cherries often sink to the bottom of a cake, so down you go, with a sinking action.

A structure for a cake dance

You could be the narrator for this dance by:

▶ calling the ingredients in turn to add to the cake

▶ mixing them with your very big spoon

▶ pouring them into a tin

▶ putting the cake in a very hot oven

▶ icing and decorating the finished cake of very still children!

Or one of the children could be the baker.

▶ Finally, when the cake is done, you could all sit in a circle and cut it, taking a slice each and enjoying what it tastes like.

If possible, precede or follow this dance by making a real cake – either a Christmas cake, a cherry cake, or just a plain sponge. The children will be ready to join in and it's one of the best sequencing activities you could do!

Shop Till You Drop!

Seasonal dance – winter

Shopping is a familiar activity for most children and as Christmas and other winter festivals come near, they will be very involved in what shopping entails!

What you need

▶ carrier bags and boxes
▶ gifts and toys
▶ a book such as **Lily and the Present** by Christine Ross (Methuen Young Books)
▶ small mats or carpet tiles
▶ some chairs
▶ a tambourine or drum

Music suggestion

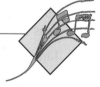

▶ **Scurry** by Brian Madigan (track 3 on the Music for Dance CD)

Action poem

▶ **Sing a Song of People** by Lois Lenski

Opening activity

Follow your chosen warm-up with this poem about people so the children can start thinking about how people move.

Sing a Song of People

Sing a song of people,
Walking fast or slow;
People in the city,
Up and down they go.

People on the pavement,
People on the bus;
People passing, passing,
In back and front of us.

People on the subway
Underneath the ground;
People riding taxis,
Round and round and round.

People walking singly,
People in a crowd;
People saying nothing,
People talking loud.

People laughing, smiling,
Grumpy people too;
People who just hurry,
And never look at you!

Sing a song of people,
Who like to come and go;
Sing of city people,
You see but never know!

Poems like this benefit from a second reading, and children may like to close their eyes so they can imagine all the different people.

Setting the scene for the dance

Begin by gathering the children together and chatting about how preparations for the festival season are going in their house. Include other festivals, such as Diwali, in your conversation.

▶ Are your parents very busy preparing for visitors and is everyone writing present lists?

▶ Does anyone know how many shopping days there are until the holiday?

▶ Time is running out and we all need to head for the high street in the Christmas rush to get the last few things organised. The dance today is going to be about the Christmas crush, the hustle and bustle and hurly burly of Christmas shopping!

Rushing, rushing, rushing! (you could use a drum for this activity)

- First you need to work on different pathways and floor patterns. You need to be able to walk at different speeds and 'freeze' when you hear me bang on the drum.
- Follow me to the shops. We are going to begin by hurrying up and down the busy high street. We must keep on the pavement and walk briskly, but we mustn't run as we might knock over other people. When you hear my bell/drum/tambourine, you must stop suddenly and look at your watch to see what the time is. It's getting very late and there is still a lot to do!
- Now follow me in a hurrying zigzag pattern to avoid bumping into the other shoppers on the high street. We may have to turn sharply to miss the people, so watch carefully!
- Now we are coming to a wriggly bit of the high street where we need to follow the pavement round in a curving pattern.
- And at last, here is the store we need. Let's go in through the revolving door. Follow me and we will all go through in a line.

In the shop

- Now we are in the shop, we need to look at our lists to see what we need.
- Can you see that beautiful scarf at the bottom of the display? Wouldn't that be perfect for Charlie's Grandma? Let's see if we can reach over to get it.
- Now jump up to reach that box of crackers on the top shelf.
- Balance on one leg as you reach to the side for that ornament for your mum – mind you don't drop it.
- Twist round – is that your friend you can hear calling you?
- Reach down to the floor to pick up someone's car keys that they have dropped on the floor.
- Mind you don't trip over that push chair coming round the corner.

Older children might enjoy developing a repetitive 'shopping pattern' by linking a few of these ideas and repeating them.

Everybody wants it!

▶ Now we need that special toy that everyone wants, and there is only one left! We must have it! Don't let that other person get it!
Describe something that everyone wants – a TV character, a computer game etc. Talk about how people behave when they all want the same thing and there are not enough!
Have a tussle, but without touching anyone else.
Try some cross and disappointed faces and body poses.

Going home at last!

▶ The shopping bags are full and they are very heavy. They feel heavier with every step we take.

▶ Come on, pick up your bags. Soften your knees and round your back and shoulders as you pick up the heavy bags.

▶ Try walking a few steps. As you move, your arms feel longer and your legs feel shorter as they buckle under the strain. Show how tired you feel by using tired expressions.

▶ It might be easier to get the bus home. Let's make a bus with chairs. We need someone to be the driver, so we can get on the bus with all our parcels.

▶ On our journey home we go:

  ▷ over a bumpy road where we bounce up and down, shake and shudder

  ▷ down a bendy road where we lean left and right as we go round the corners

  ▷ up a steep hill where we lean back into our seats, past the pond where we look out to see the ducks, and at last, we stop at our bus stop.

▶ Now we can stagger to our house with all our bags and boxes.

▶ We can put all the presents under the Christmas tree, have a cup of tea and then go straight to bed for a good rest.

Christmas Cracker

Seasonal dance – winter

> This session can build on the work from 'Shop Till You Drop!'. The toys emerging from the crackers could be those in the parcels the shoppers left under the tree.

What you need
- a Christmas cracker
- tree and other decorations, such as a Christmas fairy, a bauble, a toy soldier and a spinning top
- a book such as **The Night Before Christmas** by Clement C Moore
- small mats or carpet tiles
- a tambourine

Music suggestion
- Christmas music, carols etc.

Action poems
- Verses from The Night Before Christmas

Opening activity

Start your session with this section of the famous poem.

The Night Before Christmas

'Twas the night before Christmas,
When all through the house,
Not a creature was stirring,
Not even a mouse.
The stockings were hung
By the chimney with care
In hope that Saint Nicolas
Soon would be there.
The children were nestled
All safe in their beds,

While visions of sugar plums
Danced in their heads.
And Mama in her kercheif
And I in my cap;
Had settled our brains
For a long winter nap
When out on the lawn
There arose such a clatter
I sprang from my bed to see what
Was the matter.

(This is just the beginning of a much longer poem.)

Setting the scene for the dance

What do you think?

Help the children to create a twig tree by putting a few twigs in a vase and hanging some small decorations from it. You could tie on a few mini crackers, or some small baubles that might appeal to the children. Gather the children around the little festive tree and talk about the objects. Ask if any of them have ever pulled a Christmas cracker and talk about the little surprises they found inside. Explain that today's idea is about Christmas crackers and their hidden surprises.

Pulling the cracker

▶ We're going to begin by pulling the cracker.

▶ Find a friend and stand with your feet apart, holding your imaginary cracker between you with two hands.

▶ Imagine it is a big and very stubborn cracker. Begin with a gentle tug and gradually pull harder, making each movement bigger and stronger.

▶ On the third pull, the cracker finally pops and you travel away from your friend with quick running steps.

▶ Try again with a new cracker.

The Big Bang!

▷ Listen for my tambourine shaking and travel carefully in the room, making sure you fill all the spaces and don't bump into anyone.

▷ When I bang the tambourine, jump high on the spot as a cracker BANGS. See how many different shapes you can make in the air as you jump. Can you make a star, a turning jump, and a wide jump?

The toys

▷ Now we are going to be the toys in the crackers.

▷ First we can be soldiers, marching on the spot. Then we can march all over the room, turning sharply and keeping in a straight line.

▷ Next we can be a ball, rolling, bouncing, rising and falling.

▷ We could be a toy fairy dancer, turning on one leg. Look hard at one place in the room as you turn, so you don't get dizzy. Now try some different dancing movements.

▷ Now let's be a spinning top. Can you spin on the spot on your foot, your bottom or your knee? Who can spin fastest?

Say this rhyme as you spin:

I am a spinning top,
Round and round I go.
Sometimes faster, faster, faster!
Sometimes very slow.

Suggested structure for a dance

▷ Begin by making the activity a sort of game. The children travel around the room quickly and lightly as you shake the tambourine.

▷ On your signal (the banging of the tambourine), the cracker bangs and the children jump high and land low to the ground while you pretend to search the ground for the gift.

▷ You tell them which imaginary gift you have found and they perform the movement ideas practiced earlier.

▷ Repeat several times, changing the gift each time.

▷ Then you could get them to choose which toy they want to be.

▷ Older or more experienced children could work in pairs to guess each other's toys.

The Magic Carpet

A cultural dance – up, up and away!

This idea will act as a springboard to allow you to introduce cultural or creative themes by visiting different countries or imaginary lands. You could use the magic carpet as a way to set off in all the cultural dances in this section.

What you need

▶ a rug or blanket
▶ something to act as a magic wand
▶ a book such as **Molly's Magic Carpet** by Emma Fischel (Usborne)
▶ a tambourine

Music suggestion

▶ **Into the Unknown** by Brian Madigan (track 4 on the Music for Dance CD)

Action poem

▶ The Magic Carpet

Opening activity

> Follow your chosen warm-up with this simple action poem, so the children can guess what the theme of the dance is today.

The Magic Carpet

The children sit on the magic carpet and move to indicate what is happening.

We found a Magic Carpet
We tried to make it fly,
We all sat down and shouted
'Magic carpet, fly!'

But nothing ever happened
We really had a try,
We asked it very quietly
Which words would make it fly.

We all said 'Izzy Wizzy',
We all said 'Bip Bop Boo',
We all said 'Abracadabra',
We all said 'Shazam' too.

At last we all said 'Carpet,
Please take us in the air.'
And do you know, it did it,
And we flew everywhere!

Setting the scene for the dance

What do you think?

▶ Gather the group together and ask them to sit in a magic circle.

▶ Talk about the magic words from the poem. Ask if anyone has seen a magic show.

▶ Explain that you have brought along a very old carpet that might have magic powers and will take you all to lots of interesting places if the children can cast a magic spell and unlock its magical powers.

Suggested prompts:

▶ What is your favourite magic word? Is it Abracadabra, or Shazam, or Izzy wizzy, let's get busy?

▶ Let's choose one and then cast a spell together.

▶ What sort of movements could we do to help the magic?

▶ Now let's add some turns, claps and jumps.

▶ You could try 'Abra' (clap) 'ca' (slap thighs) 'dabra' (jump).

Repeat several times with increasing volume and vigour, until you've decided it's worked, then theatrically unroll your carpet.

Developing the idea

▶ Now that the carpet is ready, we need to make sure that you are all ready for the bumpy ride. You will need to be able to keep your balance and must be prepared for a bumpy landing as well.
Let's practice:

  ▷ Can you stay steady on one leg? Try staring at a fixed point in the room and making your body all tight. This will help to get rid of the wobbles. Try making different shapes while you balance. Try balancing on different parts of your body.

  ▷ The carpet is going to rise up in the sky, and it may swoop down low. Try rising and sinking like the carpet: sometimes rise slowly and drop suddenly. Also try a quick rise and a slow sink to the floor.

  ▷ You will be floating through the air. Can you give your body a light floaty feeling as if you are moving in slow motion and your fingers are all soft and gentle?

Suggested prompts for further activities:

▶ Now that we've had a brief introduction and flying lesson, we are ready to board our magic carpet.

▶ Begin on the floor and decide where you are going to sit.

▶ How are you going to get on the carpet? You might crawl or creep very softly so you don't make the carpet fly away before you are ready. If you're excited, maybe you will want to leap on.

▶ Prepare for take off, say your magic words and prepare to soar into the sky. Rise to your knees, then stand up. Be careful you don't fall!

▶ Now you can decide together where you will go.

Suggested structure for a dance

You could act as a narrator for the journey, giving the children prompts about what is happening. Ride on the magic carpet with them and try some of these:

▶ Rising, balancing, tipping right and left.
  Repeat, changing speed and the body part chosen to balance on.

▶ Gentle floating – a bit of soft arm flapping like a bird soaring.

▶ A sudden drop to the floor to avoid low flying birds and planes.

▶ Twisting movements to look behind and admire the view.

▶ Deliberate wobbles as the carpet hits a gust of wind.

▶ Looking in different directions at different points of interest.

▶ At last you spot your destination and the carpet is getting lower as you sink to the ground. Begin to describe what you see and ask where they think you may have landed. Give some information about the country or magical land you are visiting.

▶ Prepare for a bumpy landing perhaps sway and softly tumble to the ground.

▶ Finally, roll gently off your carpet in a dazed state and ask – 'Where are we?'

African Greeting

A circle dance from Africa

This is the first of the section of dances with cultural themes. This one uses movements of African animals and African dancing.

What you need

- small world African animals – lion, giraffe, elephant, zebra etc.
- books such as **A Triangle for Adaora** and **One Big Family** by Ifeoma Onyefulu

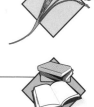

Music suggestion

- **African Greetings** by Brian Madigan (track 5 on the Music for Dance CD)

Action poem

- Africa!

Opening activity

Follow your chosen warm-up with this action poem about African animals. Tell the children you are going to a different place today and ask them if they can guess where it is as you say the poem.

Africa!

Say the poem, then repeat it with the actions.

Giraffes are tall with necks so long,
On tiptoe, arms stretched above head
Elephants' trunks are big and strong.
Bend forward, arms down, hands together, swaying
Zebras have stripes and can gallop away,
Gallop around

While monkeys in the trees do sway.
Move from tree to tree with a swaying movement
Old crocodile swims in the pool so deep,
Lie on the ground and swim
Or lies in the sun and goes to sleep.
Sleep

Setting the scene for the dance

Suggested prompts:

▶ Today we are going to find out about a different place in the world.

▶ It's a very warm place and lots of interesting animals live there. Some of them are animals you see in the zoo.

▶ Can anyone guess which country it might be?

▶ Has anyone been there?

▶ What would it be like to live in a very hot country? What would you wear?

Developing the idea

Here are some simple movement ideas that work well with the rhythmical drumming music on the CD. Try a selection of them or devise your own, and then link them into a dance structure that works for you. The ideas are built around walking, clapping, turning and changing levels.

1. Can you make sounds with different parts of your body, like this?

Clap your hands like this	Clap steadily four times.
Slap your legs like this.	Gently slap thighs with softly bent knees.
Stamp your feet like this	Stamp alternative feet four times.
As you stamp your feet imagine you are wiping a huge table in front of your body with your right arm	Stamp your feet as you turn around in a circle arriving back where you started after four steps.

2. In some parts of Africa, people may have to walk a long way to get water from a well. Let's practice some movements that show us getting water from a well.

3. Start in a crouched position and walk four steps forwards, gradually getting taller and taller. As you walk, bring your arms forward from low to high. Retreat, go backwards for four steps, clapping four claps in time with your steps.

For older or more experienced dancers:

▶ Practice walking around in a group circle, keeping your steps in time. Try clapping low into the centre of the circle and high to the outside of the circle. Make a pattern, maybe two low then two high. Try different combinations.

▶ Stand still and clap quickly from side to side as you lower yourself to the ground in a kneeling position. Make a rhythmical pattern by slapping the floor and your thighs; try long and short sounds e.g. 'short, short, long' (slap on floor, floor, clap). Try to establish a set pattern that everyone can manage.

Ideas for a dance structure

1. This sequence should work with the music suggested but could easily be adapted to most rhythmical drum music with a steady tempo. Listen to the track before you start dancing!

2. Try table wiping with one arm only, right then left (four beats each).

3. Clap hands four times,
   Slap thighs four times,
   Stamp feet four times,
   Slap thighs four times together with stamping feet.

4. Turn, taking four steps as you repeat the wiping table gesture (right hand only).

5. Repeat this until the music changes to a new phrase, four times in total.

6. Start in a circle, crouch low and walk to the middle of the circle, gradually getting taller as your arms sweep upwards. Walk backwards out of the circle for four, clapping your hands as you go.
   Repeat this motif until the music changes to a fast drumming pattern.

7. For the fast drumming section, begin by clapping quickly either side of your body as you lower yourself to a kneeling position on the ground. Involve the hips in a swaying action as you sink to the floor.

   Then choose from the following ideas:
   ▶ Make rhythmical patterns using hands, thighs and floor.
   ▶ Walk on your knees in an 'Aylesbury duck' style – walk forward, then stand and walk backwards on your feet till you are out of the circle, leading with your bottom and swaying your hips.

   ▶ While kneeling and keeping your knees together, step one knee to the side and lean over to that side, close to centre with two claps, then repeat on the other side.

   ▶ Use any of the movement ideas tried earlier.

8. To finish this section, use the fast clapping from side to side.

9. Break from the circle and create a long snaking line. The leader starts a clapping pattern, two low on one side of the body, then one high on the other side. The group follow and walk in rhythm following the leader. The leader can make a change of direction, of clapping pattern or let someone else take the lead.

Pow Wow

A cultural dance – with Native American Indian influences

This sequence uses movements historically associated with Native American Indians. You could fly to America on the magic carpet, which would give you a chance to look at other parts of America and discuss how vast and varied it is.

What you need

▶ a drum

▶ strips of card and felt pens to make simple headbands

▶ books such as **Hiawatha and Megissogwon** (National Geographic)

Music suggestion

▶ **Pow wow by** Brian Madigan (track 6 on the Music for Dance CD)

Action poem

▶ Ten Little Indians

Opening activity

Follow your chosen warm-up with this simple action poem so the children can think about the theme for today.

Ten Little Indians

Choose ten children to stand in a line as the American Indian children.

Start with the children sitting in a row.

One little, two little, three little Indians,

Four little, five little, six little Indians,

Seven little, eight little, nine little Indians,

Ten little Indian braves. HOW!

As you say the rhyme, the children stand up in turn.

Now say the verse in reverse.

Ten little, nine little, eight little Indians,

Seven little, six little, five little Indians,

Four little, three little, two little Indians,

One little Indian brave.

As you say the rhyme, the children sit down again in turn.

You could sing the song several times so all the children can have a turn at being an Indian brave.

Developing the idea

1. Ask the children to form a circle and sit down on the ground.
   Get the children to listen to the music track. Show them how to tap out the beat of the music.

2. Children should start by tapping on their legs for a count of eight.

3. When the children can manage this, they could try starting by:

   ▶ tapping their legs twice

   ▶ clapping their hands twice

   ▶ tapping their shoulders twice

   ▶ then back to their legs twice again.

4. Now try starting in a sitting position and keeping up the steady beat of clapping as they move onto their knees and then to standing. Move together, going round in a circle and changing direction, still clapping.

5. Stop the music while you sing or chant 'Land of the Silver Birch'.

   Land of the Silver Birch
   Move round in a circle

   Home of the beaver
   Change direction

   Where still the mighty moose wanders at will
   Open the fingers and make the hands form the antlers of the moose

   Blue lake and rocky shore
   Make the arms move successively from side to side to create water

   I will come back once more
   Make the arms move successively from side to side to create water

   Boom, diddy, ah-da, boom diddy ah-da,
   Fold your arms and bow

   Boom diddy ah-day, bo-oo-oom.
   Fold your arms and bow.

6. Play the music and return to the initial sequence. Some children could use simple shakers, drums or bells as they dance.

It is interesting to see if the children can pick up the rhythm of the music using the drum. Some children have a natural sense of rhythm and this exercise is a useful way to identify those who can hold a steady beat.

The Dancing Dragon

A cultural dance – inspired by Chinese New Year

This is a popular theme around the time of the Chinese New Year. You could begin the session with a 'magic carpet' ride and travel across the world to China. You could make a dragon costume with the children before the dance session. Sewing some hoops inside the fabric for the body will make it easier for the dancers to manage.

What you need

- a dragon's head made from a cardboard box
- a long piece of fabric for the dragon's body
- percussion instruments
- books such as **Moonbeams, Dumplings and Dragon Boats** by Nina Simonds (Gulliver)

Music suggestion

- **Dragon Dance** by Brian Madigan, (track 7 on the Music for Dance CD)

Action poem

- The Dragon

Opening activity

Follow your chosen warm-up with the action poem so the children can guess what the dance is today.

The Dragon

Say the rhyme holding up the dance props. Later, you could say the poem again with the children inside the dragon costume.

Here is the dragon's great big head,
And here is the dragon's body.
Look underneath at all those feet,
Do you recognise somebody?
Under the dragon's great big head,
Is Megan who helped to make him.
And under the dragon's body are
All the rest of the children.

Here comes the dragon, making a noise,
Crashing and banging and calling,
And here are the children who join in the dance,
Who help him and stop him falling.

Setting the scene for the dance

What do you think?

Explain to the children that it is tradition during the Chinese New Year to have lion and dragon dances. Lions and dragons are symbols of good luck and bring good luck to families, shops, restaurants and businesses. The dance is accompanied by loud music played on a large drum. It is believed that noise will get rid of evil. The dragon pretends to eat Chinese greens and he takes a red envelope full of money. This is the way the dragon shows that it brings good luck.

1. Begin with the children in a space of their own. Encourage them to move like the dragon in undulating movements, moving up and down on the spot.
2. Now work on different pathways. Can the children make curved, straight and zigzag pathways?
3. Try putting ideas 1 and 2 together in a dance path with undulating movements.
4. Work on developing the idea of reaching higher and higher, and lower and lower.
5. Encourage the children to use jerky movements, looking in different directions.
6. Now help the children to put the ideas together to make a short dance.

Developing the idea

▷ Depending on the size of the group, divide the children into small groups so that each group can make their own dragon. The children form a line one behind the other, holding on to the child in front by their waist. The front child is the head of the dragon and should take the lead.

▷ Encourage the children to incorporate the ideas they worked on earlier in the session, travelling in the space using different pathways, using undulating movements, changing levels, staying on the spot and using jerky movements to look in different directions.
Give the children turns at being the leader.

Creating a dance

1. Let each group take it in turns to be the dragon.

2. Put the head on the child in front. Make sure that the child can see, and that their movement and view are not restricted.

3. The other children go under the cloth, lifting it high using the hoops. Each group has a turn making up a dragon dance using the costume. Older children could be encouraged to build the dance into a climax with the dragon reaching up to the cabbage at the end.

4. Other children can join in by using percussion instruments to add to the music. Encourage the children to begin slowly and build up the rhythm in to a climax.

Rama and Sita

A cultural dance – from India

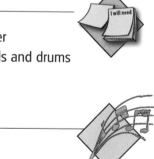

This dance is a response to the Diwali story of Rama and Sita who were banished from their country, and return, led back by the lights (divas) put out by the people of their kingdom to light the way home.

What you need

- ▶ a large piece of lightweight blue material for the river
- ▶ percussion instruments, such as bells, finger cymbals and drums
- ▶ any retelling of the story of Rama and Sita

Music suggestion

- ▶ Music from India or Pakistan would be useful (but not essential) as background

Action poem

- ▶ Little Lights

Opening activity

Follow your chosen warm-up with this simple action poem so the children can get into the mood!

Little Lights

Say the rhyme once, then say it again, adding the actions as described.

Let us make some diva lamps
To show the way back home.
Following the little lights
We will see them come.

Put the lights along the path
Showing them the way,
When they see the little lights
They will know the way.

Come and light the little lights
Light each with a flame,
When we see them coming home
We will shout their names.

Can you see the little lights
Showing the way home?
We have helped our special friends
To find their way back home.

Begin by introducing and reading the story. The story is about Prince Rama and Princess Sita who are banished from their kingdom for 14 years. After many adventures they return triumphantly. The people of the kingdom light the way with diva lights so that Rama and Sita can see their way back to the palace. Hindu and Sikh people celebrate this story every year at Diwali, the celebration of light.

Setting the scene for the dance
For younger children

What do you think?

Younger children will enjoy just walking through the story, making the movements as you retell the story line. They will enjoy the chance to be all the characters and play the whole story in a simple dance.

For older or more experienced dancers

Older and more experienced children may enjoy a more 'choreographed' version, with you as the narrator and the children coming in turn to play different characters. Here is the story sequence.

1. Once there was a good king called King Dasharatha. All the people in his country loved him.

2. The King had three wives but they were all sad because they didn't have a son to rule the land after him. The King prayed to the gods and eventually he was blessed with four sons: Rama, Bharata, Lakshmana and Shatrugnha.

3. Rama grew to be a fine prince. He met and fell in love with a beautiful princess called Sita. They had a splendid wedding. All the people came to the wedding.

4. King Dasharatha now felt he was getting too old to rule the kingdom and wanted to make Rama king.

5. But Queen Kaikeyi wanted the King to make her son, Bharata, king. A long time before, Queen Kaikeyi had saved the King's life and he had promised her two wishes in return. Now she reminded him of his promise.

6. Her first wish was that Bharata would became king, and her second wish was that the old King would send Rama away from the kingdom to live in a wild place for 14 years – and that is what happened.

7. King Dasharatha had to keep his promise, so Rama left the kingdom with Sita by his side. The third brother, Lakshmana, decided to go with Rama to take care of him.

The children could act out this part with the three characters leaving the scene. A crowd waves goodbye to them as they cross the stream and go off into the wild. Use the blue material to symbolise the stream, with children at both ends making it move gently up and down to give the impression of water. (More over the page!)

8. The three friends lived in the forest and made friends with all the creatures there. They were happy together until Ravana, the ten-headed demon king, heard about the beautiful Princess Sita. Ravana made plans to capture her.

Ten children can be the ten-headed demon, Ravana, and capture Sita and carry her away.

9. Rama was horrified when he discovered that Sita had been taken. He and Lakshmana went in search of her.

The two brothers could travel using gestures to show that they are searching for Sita.

10. Rama and Lakshmana went to the land of the Monkey-People where they meet Hanuman, the general of the monkeys. Hanuman promised that he would help them to find Sita.

The children could play the parts of the monkeys with one child being chosen as the General, Hanuman. As they dance, they could show how they become friends with the brothers and all search for Sita.

11. During their search, Hanuman met a wise eagle that told him that he had seen Ravana carry Sita across the sea between India and Sri Lanka.

The group could think about how the eagle would move. Improvise ways in which the eagle would fly and swoop down. This could produce some lovely ideas from the children. Choose a child to play the part of the eagle.

12. The monkeys and the brothers went in search of Sita. They went to the sea where they had to cross the water. The monkeys formed a bridge over the sea for the brothers to cross.

Suggest to the children that they make a bridge together. You could also use the blue material to suggest the sea.

13. The monkeys and the brothers found Ravana. A huge battle took place and Ravana was eventually killed.

The children could perform this part by making poses of the army shooting bows and arrows, holding positions and then changing them on your count. This could be effective as a group position that changed three times.

14. Sita was rescued and everyone celebrated. Rama decided that as 14 years had passed they could return home to the kingdom. The monkey people helped them on their way. Again they made a bridge so that Rama, Sita and Lakshmana could cross the water to India.

Repeat the dance phrase developed earlier.

15. The three travelled back to the kingdom and took Hanuman with them. All the people of the kingdom welcomed their return, they lined the streets with their divas alight to show the way. Later they celebrated with great feasts. They prepared to crown Rama as king and Sita as queen.

Ask the children to make two lines for the characters to walk between. The children should hold out their hands to show they are holding the divas. The children could then dance in a circle around the characters to symbolise the celebration. Finally, they could crown Rama and Sita with flowers and bow down to their new king and queen.

Creating a more complex dance

After exploring the ideas in the story, you could use them to make a dance. Tell the story again with the children re-enacting it as you go. The important thing is to encourage the flow of ideas as you go through the story, not to create a polished 'performance'.

It's the Bear!

A dance sequence inspired by The Bear Hunt

A good starting point for a dance is a story or poem. This one, following **The Bear Hunt** story by Michael Rosen, has plenty of opportunities for movement with strong facial and body expressions.

What you need

- a teddy bear
- a blanket
- a play tunnel or tents and cones
- a map
- an expedition rucksack with suitable contents
- a scarf
- **The Bear Hunt** by Michael Rosen

Music suggestion

- **Drum Talk** by Brian Madigan (track 13 on the Music for Dance CD)

Action poem

- On Tiptoe

Opening activity

Follow your chosen warm-up with this movement rhyme. Say it several times so the children are well warmed-up for the expedition.

On Tiptoe

Say the rhyme once, then say it again doing the actions as described.

When I walk on tiptoe,
It makes me feel so tall.
When I crouch down low,
I feel so very small.
But what I like
The best of all (hesitate a while)
Is to bounce, bounce, bounce,
Like a great big ball.

Follow the actions in the poem.

Setting the scene for the dance

What do you think?

▷ Begin by explaining to the children that the activity they are doing today is going to require them to walk very very quietly on tiptoes and also to crouch very low to the ground. They might also have to jump high –an they guess why they may need to do this? Where do they think they are going?

▷ Now ask a few individuals to take an item out of the rucksack. Look at the objects –a map, some binoculars, a compass and a hat etc.

▷ Introduce the idea of an expedition or an adventure. Explain that before they set off into unknown territory, it is essential that they are well prepared for all the dangers they might meet. They need to take part in some expedition training before they leave to make sure they are fit enough to go.
Are they brave enough? Are they strong enough?

Expedition training

Follow the leader

You must follow me at all times, so I know where you are. You need to do this very quietly so that we don't disturb the wild animals. Can you follow me on your tiptoes, treading very quietly and carefully? You need to practice this with a friend – take it in turns to be the leader and travel around the room. Every now and again you are going to come to a danger if you hear me shout **'It's the bear!'**, stop in your tracks and freeze until the danger passes. Let's try that a few times.

Tall wavy grass

There are parts of this forest where very tall tickly grass grows. It's taller than you and taller than me. As it sways in the breeze it makes this noise **swishy swashy, swishy swashy**, and this is how it moves: Sway from side to side with arms stretched over your head. Can you show me how the grass moves and sounds?

Now when we come across it we have to push through it with our arms powering through the long grass. It's quite tough so you have to be pretty strong to get through.

Let's try together.

Demonstrate the slashing action and encourage swishy, swashy sounds with each stroke.

Under, over and through

During our journey, we may come across a fallen tree, a stream or maybe some hollow tree trunks to crawl through. I need to see if you can cope with these obstacles.

You need to get through by moving under, over and through the objects as quickly and quietly as possible.

You could set up a small circuit of three or four stations using a tunnel, chairs, bamboo canes etc. to encourage the actions. You could also ask them to leap from stone to stone in a stream.

The echo

Does anyone know what an echo is? When we are exploring in the forest, we may have to tiptoe into a dark gloomy cave and we will probably hear our voices echo as the sound bounces off the walls. Could you be my echo?
Lets try it – **'Look over there!'** Now you say it and point where I do. Now let's practice our tiptoeing again but when I shout 'Look over there!' – you must be my echo, freeze and copy the statue shape that I make. Let's try it.

Thick oozy mud

In some parts of the forest, it is very boggy, like quicksand. As you trample through in your wellies it will feel like you are walking in treacle. The mud will make a **squelch, squelch** kind of a sound. Try to make that sound as you trudge slowly through the sticky sludge.

Creating a dance

▶ Let the children help you to construct a dark gloomy cave complete with resident bear. You could use a pop-up tent, a table with a sheet or old curtain draped over it, or some drapes to make a dark corner in your room.

▶ Set up your music player with some rhythmical music with a strong beat and start the chant.

1. Whisper **'We're going on a bear hunt'** as the group are gathered around you.
Repeat the phrase over and over as you gradually stand up and begin to form a circle, increasing the volume of the chant. Let the children follow you in a circle formation as they chant **'We're going on a bear hunt'**.

2. After a few repetitions, add slapping thighs to the rhythm of the chant and try walking with a change of levels; two low steps then two high. You could add a change of direction, break the circle and walk forwards and backwards as a group, or take them to different areas in the space as you continue to chant.

3. Change the chant to **'We're going to catch a big one'**. As you speak the words, take two steps forwards then jump, landing on two feet as you 'roar' and hold up your claws! Repeat several times until the group are copying and joining in.

4. Change the chant to **'What a beautiful day'**. As you speak the words, rise onto the balls of your feet, stretch upwards and open out your arms. Repeat several times.

5. Change the chant to **'We're not scared... well just a little!'** As you speak the words, stamp your feet defiantly, then shiver as you say, '... **just a little!'**

6. Change the chant to **'Look, over there!'** As you speak the words, freeze and point to different areas in the room. The children must copy your pose and respond with an echo. Repeat four times.

7. Change the chant to **'Uh oh, long wavy grass!'** As you speak the words, represent the grass by waving your hands from high to low as you say 'wavy'. Repeat the phrase several times. Continue saying **'Can't go over it, can't go under it, gotta go through it'**. Use gestures to demonstrate each of the actions.

8. Now use the **'swishy swashy'** action practiced earlier to tackle the tall grass, chanting the phrase as you go along.

9. Change the chant to **'Uh oh! Mud, thick oozy mud... we can't go over it, can't go under it, gotta go through it'**. Use gestures to demonstrate the under, over and through actions.
Now use the **'squelch squelch'** action practiced earlier when 'walking in treacle' as you chant the phrase.

10. Finally, call out **'Look over there, a cave, a dark gloomy cave'**. Gather the group together and discuss whether they are brave enough to investigate.
If they are, begin tiptoeing towards the 'cave'. Explain that as the expedition leader, you must go first to look inside the cave. As you peek gingerly through the opening to your cave, report back: **'One shiny wet nose, two fluffy brown ears, two big googly eyes ... it's a bear! Let's run!'** The group all scatter and run off. After further discussion with the group, persuade them that he looked quite friendly and that if you all went together, it might be alright. Persuade a volunteer to investigate and they could unveil a cuddly teddy bear complete with a jar of honey!

Or

The bear might be really fierce, and then you will need to go:
back through
the oozy mud,
the swishy grass,
the splashy stream,
back to your home where you slam the door,
run upstairs and hide under the bedclothes!

Butterfly Dance

A dance sequence inspired by **The Very Hungry Caterpillar**

> This dance is one of a series that you could develop, covering life cycles of familiar animals, insects and other creatures – you could try frogspawn to frog, egg to chicken, baby to grandparent etc.

What you need

▶ pictures or small world versions of the stages of development of a butterfly

▶ a parachute or large piece of lightweight fabric

▶ the book **The Very Hungry Caterpillar** by Eric Carle (Puffin)

Music suggestion

▶ **Papillon** by Brian Madigan (track 8 on the Music for Dance CD)

Action poem

▶ Frogs Jump by Evelyn Bayer

Opening activity

Follow your chosen warm-up with this movement rhyme about animal movements. Say it several times so the children are well warmed-up.

Frogs Jump

Say the rhyme once, then say it again, doing the actions described.

Frogs jump, caterpillars hump,
Worms wriggle, insects tiggle,
Rabbits hop, horses clop,
Snakes slide, seagulls glide,
Mice creep, deer leap,
Puppies bounce, kittens pounce,
Lions stalk ... but I walk!

Setting the scene for the dance

What do you think?

▶ Begin by reading the story of **The Very Hungry Caterpillar**. Show the children the pictures or small versions and ask them to help you to put them in the correct sequence in a line and then in a circle.

▶ Use the children to demonstrate the cycle by choosing a child to represent the egg, a small caterpillar, a large caterpillar, a chrysalis and finally a butterfly.

▶ Ask these children to make these shapes in a circle formation to emphasise the ongoing nature of the cycle. Explain to the children that today they will be creating a dance based on the life cycle of a butterfly.

Developing the idea

▶ Can you find a space? Now imagine you are a tiny egg on a leaf. Curl up very small into a tight, round ball.

▶ Now imagine you are a caterpillar. Practice undulating, wavy movements along the ground. Be long and thin to begin with and then arch your back before stretching out again. Now try to move along the ground as you loop and stretch.

- Can you make the actions small for the young caterpillar and large for the huge caterpillar?

- Think about the way a caterpillar makes a cocoon, spinning silk around itself. Can you make turning, spinning actions on the spot – try not to get dizzy! Use your arms to wrap around your bodies to make a cocoon.

- Now stay still in your cocoon. You are changing into a butterfly. Unwrap and unfurl slowly until you emerge as a beautiful butterfly.

- Fly around the floor, being careful of the other butterflies, looking for the spaces.

- Think about how a butterfly moves. Travel in a graceful way using a floating action, using all the space as you fly, turning and using curved pathways. Sometimes flutter close to the ground and at other times reaching high on the tips of your toes. You could even do some graceful leaping.

Creating a dance

1. Begin by being the egg on the leaf. Imagine that you are going to hatch out into a tiny caterpillar. Keep your hands and arms by your side and begin to wiggle out of your shell. Slowly stretch out and change your shape from a ball into a long thin shape.

2. Keep your movements small, wiggling a little then stopping. You are a hungry caterpillar but the first thing you eat is your shell!

3. Begin to explore your surroundings and search for food. Remember how a caterpillar moves.

4. Imagine that you have found something tasty to eat. Stop and eat it, using your caterpillar jaws. Move on to find more food. After each meal, make your movements a little larger until you turn into a huge caterpillar.

5. Now you have tummy ache! Rub your tummy. Eat a tasty green leaf to make you feel better.

6. Use the turning movements we practiced earlier to make your cocoon and wrap your arms around your body. Hold that position carefully. You could provide the children with fabric, or even some pillow cases, to wrap around themselves or climb into, to add a different dimension and interest to the dance.

7. Now slowly unwrap your arms and turn in to a beautiful butterfly. Use floating, light movements, and flutter around the space and enjoy your new freedom as a butterfly.

You could use a parachute for one child to wrap themself up in. As the butterflies emerge from their cocoons, they then help to unwrap the child in the parachute. They could hold the parachute up on either side of the child so that the colours represent the butterfly wings.

A Crown for Max

A dance sequence inspired by **Where the Wild Things Are**

This dance is developed from 'Where the Wild Things Are' by Maurice Sendak. The setting is like a dream and gives plenty of scope for the imagination!

What you need

- ▶ a large piece of blue fabric for the ocean
- ▶ percussion instruments
- ▶ books **Where the Wild Things Are** by Maurice Sendak (Red Fox)

Music suggestion

- ▶ **Sport of Kings** by Brian Madigan (track 9 on the Music for Dance CD)

Action poem

- ▶ Monsters Everywhere

Opening activity

Follow your chosen warm-up with this movement rhyme about animal movement. Say it several times so the children are well warmed-up.

Monsters Everywhere

Say the rhyme once, then say it again, doing the actions described.

Monsters here and monsters there,
Monsters, monsters everywhere!
Monsters come and monsters go,
Waving sharp claws high and low.
Monsters big and monsters small,
Monsters short and monsters tall.
Monsters leap and monsters jump,
Monsters stamp and monsters thump,
I love monsters, yes I do,
I love monsters best, don't you?

Setting the scene for the dance

Explain that the activity today is to tell the story of Max and the wild things, using dance.

Developing the idea

1. Max in trouble!

Send the children to find a space of their own. Ask them if they have made mischief like Max. Imagine that the children have a wolf suit to wear and that they are going to put it on. Let them show you two naughty, cheeky faces and then run away. Build this into a dance phrase as you say, '**Funny face, funny face, run away**'.

Now go into role as Max's mum and send the children to their rooms! Ask the children to imagine how they feel all alone in their room.

2. In the forest

First we are going to make a forest. Start on the floor and gradually grow into trees. You could weave in and out of each other so that the trees become tangled. Now the trees are blowing in the wind and the wind becomes a gale. As the storm calms, your movements become gentle and slow.

3. On the ocean

Now let's work together to be the 'tumbling ocean'. Make one or two lines and move in an undulating fashion forwards and backwards. Explain to the children that the waves are coming in to the beach and then back again.

The waves are small and calm. Now they are getting bigger and bigger as the wind comes. At last the storm goes away again and the sea is calm.

Choose someone to dance the role of Max. Put him/her in the 'box boat'. Use the blue fabric for the children to create the sea. Encourage Max to move in the boat on the stormy sea. The material is even more effective if it moves over Max in the boat.

4. With the Wild Things

As Max arrives on land, we need to become **Wild Things**. Max is frightened and worried at first as the wild things **roar their terrible roars and gnash their terrible teeth, and roll their terrible eyes and show their terrible claws,** The movements here are a straight interpretation of the text.

Max soon calms their monster antics by staring into their eyes and shouting **Be Still!**

The Wild Things are so impressed with Max that they make him King of the Wild Things. The Wild Things can make ceremonious movements as they crown Max and bow down to him.

5. The Wild Rumpus

Max says **Let the Wild Rumpus start!** We can all do the Wild Rumpus dance together. You can dance with a partner and swing each other round, dance on your own or make up a new dance routine.

Then Max stops the party and sends the Wild Things to bed. He is lonely now, and he begins to miss his home.
He decides to stop being King of the Wild Things.

But the Wild Things shout **Please don't go, we'll eat you up we love you so!** But Max then steps back into his boat to go home.

6. Going home

Max gets into his boat and he goes across the ocean.

He goes through the forest until at last he gets back to his home.

And as Max arrives back in his bedroom, he finds his supper and **it is still hot!**

The Shining Fish

A dance sequence inspired by The Rainbow Fish

The Rainbow Fish is another story that lends itself to a dance sequence. It has a clear story line and a variety of characters to encourage a range of movements and dance sessions.

What you need

▶ big sequins threaded on a string for fish scales
▶ a big piece of lightweight blue fabric for the ocean
▶ percussion instruments
▶ the book **The Rainbow Fish** by Marcus Pfister

Music suggestion

▶ **Waterfall** by Brian Madigan (track 10 on the Music for Dance CD)

Action poem

▶ The Fisherman from **This Little Puffin**

Opening activity

You can use this stretching rhyme as a warm-up activity. Say it several times so the children are gently stretched and ready to move.

The Fisherman

Say the rhyme once, then say it again, doing the actions described.

The fisherman rows his boat to sea,
To fetch some fish for his children's tea.
He throws his net out in the sea
And catches fish for you and me.

Sit in a circle and as you say 'he throws his net', stretch out as far as possible in front to throw the net. Then pull the net towards you as you say the last line.

Setting the scene for the dance

What do you think?

▶ Begin by reading the story. The story tells the tale of a beautiful fish who has wonderful scales but will not share with the other fish. She asks the advice of the Starfish and the Octopus who advise the fish to share, then everyone is happy.

▶ Ask the children if they want to go down into the deep blue sea. Explain that they need to create the deep blue sea first of all.

We need to hold the edges of the material and move it up and down to make the waves. Begin by making small waves in the shallow water, then increase the size of the waves, as the water gets deeper.

▶ Now let's sit on the material and imagine that we are in a boat at sea. Move as if you are in a boat on calm sea and then on choppy water.

- ▷ Now we need to put on our masks so we can see the beautiful fish and the other sea creatures.
- ▷ Dive down deep into the sea and swim around looking at all the creatures that live under the sea.
- ▷ Now let's imagine we are some of the fish, moving through the water, diving, swirling, twirling and playing in the sea.
- ▷ Next, let's imagine we are the Rainbow Fish. How does the Rainbow Fish swim differently to the other fish? How can you show that you are different? Can you swim proudly with your head high, gliding by the other fish with your nose in the air?

The Rainbow Fish circle dance

1. Play a circle game as the Rainbow Fish rejects her friends. The children dance round in a circle. One child dances round the outside, refusing to join the circle. Then they dive into the middle and show off. At the end of their turn, they choose someone else to be the Rainbow Fish.

2. Create a dance phrase to show how the other fish reject the Rainbow Fish because she will not share her scales.

   The children form a line. One child is the Rainbow Fish and dances in front of the others. As they pass, each child turns away from the Rainbow Fish.

   The child playing the Rainbow Fish could wear the string of sequin 'scales' around their waist.

Working with a partner (older children)

1. Can you make a starfish shape with your body? Can you move like a starfish, keeping your shape?

2. Now try with a partner. One plays the Starfish, the other plays the Rainbow Fish.

   The Rainbow Fish travels to the Starfish and holds a position.
   The Starfish turns and then directs the Rainbow Fish away towards the octopus.
   Now change over.

3. Now practice how the Octopus would move. Try to be strong and graceful but forceful. Can you move your arms and legs like the long tentacles of an octopus?
Choose a child to play the role of the Octopus. You could have one child as the body and eight children coming out from the body on the floor, moving as tentacles.
You could make a cave out of the blue material and a table.

4. Now watch the Rainbow Fish going to the Octopus.

   Choose a child to wear the scales around their waist.

   The Rainbow Fish swims to the Octopus who moves with strong, forceful movements.

5. The Rainbow Fish swims away from the Octopus and begins to share their scales with all the other fish.

6. Now all the fish swim happily together! Swim around with all the other fish. Choose which sort of fish you will be.

Superheroes!

A dance sequence inspired by Fantasy and superhero play

Superheroes hold a special place in children's minds and imaginations.
This dance sequence gives them a chance to play out the fantasy roles safely and with support from you.

What you need

▶ pictures of various superheroes
▶ superhero models and figures
▶ percussion instruments

Music suggestion

▶ **Spiderman** by the Ramones, or **The Incredible Hulk**, **Mission Impossible**, **Thunderbirds** etc.

Action poem

▶ Spider, spider

Opening activity

Follow your chosen warm-up with this stretching rhyme. Say it several times so the children have loosened up their hands and fingers.

Spider, spider

Say the rhyme once, then say it again, with the actions described.

Spider hurrying,
Spider scurrying,
(Run fingers back and forth)
See her silken thread.
(Stretch imaginary thread between forefingers and thumbs.)
Spider hurrying,
Spider scurrying,
(Run fingers back and forth)
See her little web!
(Make spiral with forefingers.)

Setting the scene for the dance

▶ We began today with an action poem about a small creature with eight legs who probably lives in your house and certainly lives in mine. Some grown ups are quite scared of them.

▶ There's a TV character who is like a spider – do you know his name? Do you know any other superheroes?

▶ Superheroes are very strong and brave, and they always do things to help other people.

▶ Today, Spiderman is going to be the hero of our dance.

Developing the idea

Begin by talking about the story. Why does he change into a spider? What special powers does he have? He can grip and climb; he can go upside down; he can spin a web that he releases from his hands; and he can swing from the threads he spins.

Imagine that when you were sound asleep in bed last night, an incy wincy teeny weeny spider nibbled your toe and when you woke up, you had been given Spiderman's special powers!

1. **Iron grip**

   Suddenly your hands are made of magnets and you can stick to anything. Begin in a crouched position and stretch each arm out to the side and grasp the imaginary wall in front of you with your magnet hands. Make your fingers really stiff and pointy. Gradually rise as you 'climb' the wall in front of you, reaching in different directions above and to the side of your body.

2. **Upside down**

   Now think about how you can go upside down. Look at other people and try their ideas too.

3. **Spinning a web**

   With clenched fists, roll your hands quickly round each other like we do in 'Wind the bobbin up'. Then pretend to release the thread from each hand with a good sound effect.

   Older children could try making a group web where they link hands and weave in and out of each other and turn under in the manner of 'In and Out the Dusty Bluebells'.

4. **Swing and turn**

   Circle an arm with increasing speed, then swing from the thread as you run and jump with a half turn to face the direction you have just come from.

5. **Spider scurrying**

   Try travelling sideways but facing the front with a slipping, sliding movement. As you move, shoot your hands out in all directions in a spidery way. Do it again, going back the way you came.

6. Spider combat (this needs practice!)

Spiderman often ends up fighting the baddies and while he is punching and karate kicking, he uses special words to describe his moves! With strong and powerful actions, try punching the air while you shout some of his favourite words, such as: Whomp! Thwomp! Schwackk! Schwash! Can you make up some more power words? Remind the children that they mustn't touch anyone else as they fight.

Creating a dance

The music suggested is very fast and furious and also quite short.
Here are some movements you could use to construct a simple dance sequence.

▶ Crouch in a pose copied from the story, then move in a climbing action from low to high.

▶ Spider scurry, travelling from side to side.

▶ Swing and turn.

▶ Spin a web on your own and send out threads from both hands and feet.

▶ Make a group or individual web.

▶ Break out of the web to answer a distress call – use karate movements and Spiderman speak e.g. 'Thwomp' etc.

▶ Move upside down.

Use repetition of some of the phrases to use the length of the music.

There are a number of other superheroes who have movement potential. Cat Woman, Wonder Woman, Batman, The Incredible Hulk, Superman, Flash Gordon, The Bionic Man and Woman all offer possibilities.

You could also develop your own characters with special powers suggested by the children. Butterfly Girl, Dragonfly Boy and Snake Man could all inhabit your dances, rescuing people from danger and conquering the baddies!

Using different stimuli

Here are some ideas for sounds, objects and other items to enhance discussion and give children ideas for dance and movement.

Sense, sound and listening

Music
Percussion
Poetry
Voice
Stories
Action rhymes
Action/movement words
Chants
Rap
Calls, shouts, whistles and whispers

Sense vision

Paintings/pictures
Sculpture
Cartoon characters
Photographs
Toys
Animals
Nature
Weather
Machines
Natural/made objects

Sense touch

Fabrics

Natural objects such as fruit, seed heads, nuts and leaves, bark, feathers, fur, stones and shells

Malleable materials such as gloop, slime, cornflour and cooked spaghetti

Physical props to move with

Hoops
Lycra fabric
Ribbon sticks
Elastic
Balls
Balloons
Scarves
Net
Foil
Parachute

Useful books and resources

Children dancing; Rosamund Shreeves; Ward Lock Educational

Jabadao Dance Organisation has resources, books and courses for all ages including the Early Years:
Branch House
18 Branch Road
Armley, Leeds, LS12 3AQ
Tel. 0113 231 0650
Fax. 0113 263 5863
info@jabadao.org

Helping Young Children with Steady Beat; Ros Bayley
Helping Young Children to Imagine; Ros Bayley
Helping Young Children to Think Creatively; Ros Bayley

all from Lawrence Publications
17 Redruth Road,
Walsall, West Midlands, WS5 3EJ
Tel. 01922 643833
Fax. 01922 643 833
www.educationalpublications.com

Bobby Shaftoe, Clap your Hands; Sue Nicholls; A&C Black

Three Tapping Teddies; Kaye Umansky; A&C Black

Brian Madigan
Brian composed and recorded the music on the Dance CD.
You can contact him at:
brian@brianmadigan.de
www.brianmadigan.de
Madmusik, Adalbert-Stifter-Strasse 7,
83404 Ainring,
Deutschland
tel: +49 (0)8654 776153

CD tracks

Track 1 – Awakening (Roots and Shoots; Splash Dance)

Track 2 – Rainy Day (Autumn Weather)

Track 3 – Scurry (Shop Till You Drop!)

Track 4 – Into the Unknown (The Magic Carpet)

Track 5 – African Greetings (African Greetings)

Track 6 – Pow wow (Pow wow)

Track 7 – Dragon Dance (Dragon Dance)

Track 8 – Papillon (Butterfly Dance)

Track 9 – Sport of Kings (A Crown for Max)

Track 10 – Waterfall (Rainbow Fish)

Track 11 – Sand Dance (warm-up and general use)

Track 12 – Desert Rain (warm-up and general use)

Track 13 – Drum Talk (It's the Bear!)

The Little Books Club

There is always something in Little Books to help and inspire you.
Packed full of lovely ideas, Little Books meet the need for exciting and
practical activities that are fun to do, address the Early Learning Goals
and can be followed in most settings. Everyone is a winner!

We publish 5 new Little Books a year. Little Books Club members receive
each of these 5 books as soon as they are published for a reduced price.
The subscription cost is £37.50 – a one off payment that buys
the 5 new books for £7.50 instead of £8.99 each.

In addition to this, Little Books Club Members receive:
· Free postage and packing on anything ordered from the
  Featherstone catalogue
· A 15% discount voucher upon joining which can be used to buy any
  number of books from the Featherstone catalogue
· Members price of £7.50 on any additional Little Book purchased
· A regular, free newsletter dealing with club news, special offers and
  aspects of Early Years curriculum and practice
· All new Little Books on approval - return in good condition within 30
  days and we'll refund the cost to your club account

Call 020 7440 2446 or email: littlebooks@acblack.com for
an enrolment pack. Or download an application form from our website:

www.acblack.com/featherstone

If you have found this book useful you might also like ...

LB Discovery Bottles
ISBN 978-1-9060-2971-5

LB Christmas
ISBN 978-1-9022-3364-2

LB Making Poetry
ISBN 978-1-4081-1250-2

LB Music
ISBN 978-1-9041-8754-7

All available from
www.acblack.com/featherstone/